The Dream Queen

MELANIE MCCURDIE

Copyright © 2016 Melanie McCurdie

Cover Model: Jessika Dillard
Photo by Danny Calling Chase
MorbidX Alternative Modeling

All rights reserved.
ISBN 10: 1530765080
ISBN-13: 978-1530765089

This is a work of fiction. Names, characters, businesses, places, events and incidents are either the products of the author's imagination or used in a fictitious manner. Any resemblance to actual persons, living or dead, or actual events is purely coincidental.

No part of this book, be it digital or hardcopy, may be reproduced or transmitted in any form or by any means, electronic or mechanical, including photocopying, recording or by any information storage and retrieval system, without written permission from the author.

Dedication

Thank you.

To my family
To my friends and fiends
To Muse, as always

Thank you to the lovely lady who graces the cover of Darker, The Dream Queen, Jessika Dillard of MorbidX Alternative Modeling. Also, to the talented photographer, Danny Calling Chase. My deepest appreciation to you both

Melanie McCurdie

À cœur vaillant rien d'impossible.

Nothing is impossible for a willing heart

What if

Hey you...yeah. You. Come here. Quickly!!! Jesus are you stupid?

Look up. See them circling? You think they are seagulls Surveillance for a snack. You are probably right. But - what if they aren't seagulls. What if they are pterodactyls? What if you are the snack?

And that pack of dogs? You find them distasteful and sneer. What if they aren't just a few neglected unfortunates? What if they are Hadrosaurs? Or velociraptors?

What if now isn't where you are, but someplace foreign and unreal? Uncivilised. What if you were alone?

What if?

The Last Angel

I see it all.
Each darkened corner full of monsters and pixie dust
and the bodies of dead dreams piling like cordwood
under dust bunny tarps.

The nightmarish coursers that haunt my waking hours
smell like corrupted flowers and cinnamon fire; an
obscene mix that sours my stomach and comforts what
remains of my heart.

I see it all and it makes me want to simply accept fate
and fade away and I would. I would except they won't let
me go. They won't let me leave and trap me with I love
you.

I love you.

I love you...

FaDiNg TrEeS

It denotes a pattern
She notes, her pen scratching
Rats in the walls, skitter scatter
Thoughtfully, she taps her nails
And watches the breeze play in the trees
They fade, vividly waving goodbye
If only she could fade as the trees do
Only Jack Frost would miss her

Fuck You

Death is life,"
I said, as I fucked her.
I fucked her with my knife,
inserting it into her warm wet flesh.
Back and forth.
In and out,
twisting as she screams.
His breath comes faster behind me,
adding his baritone to her falsetto.
Heavenly harmony,
and music to my Master's Soul

Rats

Slithering, sniggering, sinister rats
Slinking in shadowed doorways
Always whispering behind fans and ferns
Always so unconcerned
But the itching sound of soulless claws
Giggling along the edge of darkness
Drives me batshit crazy and
Still they assume that they are invisible

Melanie McCurdie

Tainted Honey

> Obsequiousness rendered obsolete
> Eloquence is simply lost in translation
> It astounds how little one registers
> In the face of such tainted honesty
> As though the paradigm shifted and
> Reality had become a serial cannibal

The Party

Adorable anger
Your eyes like needles
Pulled into shadows
Covert kisses
The obsession rages
Covetous glances
Across the crowded room
Torturous anticipation
Goodnight wishes
You wait in the dark
And I fall to your desire

Vigil

I kept it all,
every single communication,
each word you wrote.
I kept them in a paper envelope,
wrapped in string.

For so many years I thought they were love
until one day I realized your words were knives and
that bundle on my heart was filled with half-truths

So pull the blades and sew up the holes
one by one excised flesh made nothing.
Tonight I burn a vigil

Holes

My mind has too many holes
Ladders in stalkings, passion
Some sinuous snake slithers
Trails ribbons rubbing away traces
Crimson cacophony, bells toll
Tracks, my eyes run in my mind
Round the forgotten corner
Down another silent hall
Footprints on the dusty floor
Handprints mark the rotting wall
Signs and signals point the way
Apocalyptic memory
Just to claw through the steel veil
Soul filter, like wire mesh
My mind has too many holes

Naked

Awake
Naked
Truly exposed
Not bare skinned but bare souled
Darkness embraces a new freedom
In the absence of light I can let go the masque
Forget my scars and lessons
Lost time between consciousness and careworn; the
memory of your warmth reminds me that I exist
The knowledge of your loss
Stabs me suffering life in the cold.

Faith of the Faithless

Insecurity, a common killer
The inner criminal element
Straight outta serotonin motherfucker
None of that dopamine shit neither
That nasal whiny bitch's tones
Nails across the chalkboard is sweeter
It keeps moaning shoulda, woulda, coulda
It's an old and tired litany
But it drives the point home better than a hammer
Because it's not about what I can't change
But, instead.... what if I can't —

Since You Asked

How it feels:

Fingers clawed
Quasimodo reborn
Who needs a spoon when the
Tremors stir the tea in my cup?
You could consider it a silver lining
Every nerve is on fire
It burns like napalm frostbite
Even through sweat slick palms
Pharmaceuticals be damned
I fucking hate taking them.
Stabbing myself in the eye
Would bring quicker relief
But that means effort
And I like my eye
So I'll wait

Hilarity

You want to touch me?
LOL you don't have either the balls,
nor the backbone,
or even likely the stamina.
Talk a good game, don't you hero?
All puffed up like King Kong
Ugh it's ridiculous
"You won't forget me"
Oh hell, have you considered,
That it's me YOU won't forget
Self important swagger
It really doesn't impress

Melanie McCurdie

Black Orchid

Draped like breathing silk
Ivory skin, ivory keys
Raven tresses decoration
Play me, she whispers
Eyes averted, nervous
Black Orchid
No shrinking violet, she shivers
Speak her name
Watch her fracture, smile
A heady concoction
Igneous she burns
Your hand, Eruption
Detonation: Ground Zero
Her eyes

Nectar

I hold you in my hands
Warming your flesh
Within my palms
Desiring the taste of your skin on my lips
The honeyed essence within beginning to flow
I feel the coldness seep
Through your thin rosy sheathing
Replaced by the warmth of your nectar
How l long to plunge my teeth into your taut hide
To draw forth onto my tongue your luscious juices
To consume of your body
Feed my own
Ravenous I devour
My lifeblood restored

Apple

The Lonely Succubus

Yes.
I want to feel your hands and lips
Fingertips
I want to ride you like a bike I stole
Hard and fast as I can
You think you could keep up?
Many have attempted and failed
I doubt you'd survive
I do wish you'd come closer though
It gets so lonely on my side of hell
Trapped here in need of warmth
And companionship
Someone to share my fire
Dare you, handsome
Dare you to try
I'll bleed you dry

Moonlight

You taste like moonlight and blood
Just like the night we met,
In the forest
Where we walked hand in hand
And you told me all the secrets I longed to hear
With the crickets playing a symphony
To the percussion of the darkness
That ebbed and flowed around us.
Centuries ago, yesterday
My life became forfeit
My mundane existence stolen
Volunteered, the slaughter ahead enticing
You laid me down and loved me
Imbibed me, and you tasted like moonlight

Telepathy

It's not fair
To feel you all over my body
Stealing my breath
With memories not mine
And I have no control
But respond to your kisses
The touch of your tongue
You fill me, with coldness
Icicles inside me melting
What are you doing to me?
No one has permission
Behind those locked doors
Your teeth, they hurt so good
Stop distracting me!!!
Oh I clamp down and it hurts
Because you're fading as I cum
My arms grasping to hold you
Just a moment more
Then you're gone and
I open my eyes
My pillow is wet as my pussy
And I ache.
It's not fair.

Quietude

Shhhh
No talking
Voices spoil the reality
Passion brought us here
Let's not waste words discussing
A not so secret desire
Human, you are so warm
Close enough to taste the salt of your skin
So just kiss me ~~and~~ again
So I can feel something
Feel anything but this gnawing disquiet and
The distance that grows wider
With each lecture on prowess
Each pointed verbal finger
That highlights the reasons why
Guilt should be paramount
I don't care about the reasons why
Rather, I care about the closeness
The flesh contact and eye grip
Instead of the sinking depths
That come under the definition
Of Love

Soul Synapsis

Yeah I hear you moaning
In your Emojish tongues
It's all in the vernacular
Don't you know?
There is no cure for acerbic wit
It's hardly a sickness
Twitch the bitch switch, I'm down if it is
Today, the social diction is hardly spectacular
Sadly lacking the eloquent factor
I miss the pretty words
I find, too, that my vascular capacity is next to null
I think I have a slow leak
Maybe I'm a Synapsid out of its prime
A soul Synapsis
I still love you though
In my eyes, everything is irie
We stay gold, just like Pony Boy
Like the last whit of light in the sky

Poem

I'm trying.
I know it's not enough
It's never enough
But I keep trying –
Maybe in hopes of a miracle
But I know those don't exist
I have a better chance of finding a unicorn
Take a look around you
Reality sucks balls
So maybe I'm too stupid to stop
Maybe even though I've lost my faith
I still believe that people aren't wholly evil
Journey said Don't Stop Believing
(You just sang that)
But you have to wonder if they ever did

A Scream to the Oblivious

Sometimes, you just can't win
I'd lay my life down and stand up to fight
Every fucking day of my life but
At times
It feels like
A waste of time
A waste of words to speak
A waste of precious air
One might prefer to be an apparition
For all the good a voice does
Once, I thought it'd be fun
Some kind of messed up game to be invisible
But it turns out that it sucks balls
To scream to the oblivious

Blade

It's a heartquake, of sorts.
It's devastating to find oneself inadequate.
Those little inconceivable, undeniable truths are simply
the death knell of that fundamental core.
One can shellac over the hairline fractures,
those nearly invisible scars that come taking from blow
after blow to our fragile egos
We think we are stronger for it
Beating our breasts and shouting
But the blade of inadequacy, once felt, never withdraws,
and you live with it sticking out of your chest like a
medallion
because to remove it would mean that you may die while
you breathe

Wistful

Running here
Running there
Endless questions, debates
Stop, stare out the window
Sigh quietly inside
Momentary pause
Reality bites
It screams and it howls
Suddenly I'm back again
Back in the game once more
I want to hide away.
Now in the shower, cry
Where no one else can see
Clipped daemon wings don't fly
Letting go is so hard
God I fucking hate it
Weak sister, a poor example
That's another story
It's why I weep unseen
If I weep at all

A Jokable Concept

I miss you.
It's nothing specific,
I can't really name a reason
There's nothing that makes me smile
Other then the melodic mornings
Dozy daydreams and secret laughter
It's not like I miss you near
Because you were never here
I acknowledge that investment in anything
Beyond self-gratification was null
A jokable concept
Honestly, it was so funny that I cried 'til I laughed
If anyone asks me, I'll simply deny
No, just no-one that I used to know
Then inwardly sigh
Because, you giant ass,
I do kinda miss you.

And She Knows

She knows
I've told her the way I feel
Time has passed,
I've changed, she says
And I believe her
I can see her as I knew her
That happens between decades
It happens, sometimes
But my feelings haven't changed
I'm not what I used to be
I've changed for the better
No longer battered by beer and late nights
The strings I once played
Are dust in the wind
The kid I once was is dust in her eyes
When I tell her that I love her
And she says knows

Enter The Fool

It's a consequential downfall
To being open-hearted
Passion in the field of war
Makes pitfalls prominent
It's no tiptoe through the land mines
Masquerading as wildflowers
At times it's more about maintaining silence
Rather than slicing Gordian Knot
Enter the fool and dance like hell
But hell is no place for angels
Feathers smoulder like embers
Surrounded by conformity
Every face you see
Is simply flesh for fantasy
We live in a three-dimensional world
With mental acuity that's one faceted
And still expect understand what's real

Melanie McCurdie

Sleepwaker

I know you hate it when I watch you sleep
I don't care and do it anyway,
You're not aware of my stare and its just as well
My watchful gaze makes you nervous
Gives you the creeps, were your words, as I recall
I still don't care.
Observing your eyes move behind the thin membrane
Lost in a dream, you speak foul atrocities
Fist flying in a fury of blows.
From my little lost world, I watch the fight
Helpless to end it, powerless to change the outcome
Unwilling to test fate and chance wrath
As I detest the sensitivity of purple I love yous under my skin
The ones you bring when the Demon takes control again
I prefer the sweet wine of kisses
to the bitter gall of defeat
It's no victory to lay in wait of the next skirmish
When night has fallen and
Morpheus demands my sacrifice

He

Suave
Debonair
Such savoir faire
I stare, enraptured
engaged and unable to help myself.
That's how you like it
Your romantic nature belies
Steals
Softens the suspicion while
Your smile cuts like a knife
You monster
I like it too
It's déjà vu
Not like meeting My Monster, or the Devil
They can't compete or compare.
In my eyes
nothing hurts so exquisitely well
Breathless as the charisma
that is He

La Petite Mort de Folie

I didn't mean to kill her.
They, were paintings on the wall
Just collateral damage
Her, Folie, bottle green eyes
Her, I did and with intent
It wasn't intentional
Premeditated mistake
An unplanned surgical strike
She begged for rebellion
Folie followed the shadows
Her unflappably bright smile
Fiercely shone from heartsblood stained lips
Everyone said she was sweet
Irresistible sweet treat
Writhing, she tasted of wine
Whining, she just tasted dead
Folie, her green eyes shining
Laughed, no she didn't cry out
When the shadows caressed her
Inferno in her late smile
And promises Hell and more
When I return to her
Tonight

Bipedal Crow

It's a worn out point of contention.
sigh It's plain to see that
raven wings don't hide straw.
Those fucking sparkles stand out like a sore thumb...
or a neon sign
As a breathing storage system, I collect shiny things for
review. An upright walking crow, if you will
feather shuffle
But it's a blight on my hard drive
to compile so much data.
Plight, though it is, moreover a curse, the usefulness,
eventually does reveal its beautiful binary self and, as is
common in such instances, the realisation drop kicks me
in the solar plexus and it's a K.O.
I didn't even know I was in the ring.
Mind. Blown.
The most wonderful reward for discovery,
Is that once made, everything else unnecessary
If fit for nothing more than File G
Thrown out ...Jettisoned ...Incinerated ...
Killed *rustling feathers*
To make space for more Data

Bleu

It's not enough.
It's not enough to sit and watch someone else's fingers
Plié et pirouette
Across the ivory landscapes
I want to dance and soar, fly too
Never enough ear candy to slake
That hunger, the consuming need
To sit down and pour notes from my hands
They ache for the cool keys
Vampires craving blood couldn't be more ravenous
When Gershwin cries his Rhapsody
My heart cries from the anguish
Of not being able to comply
I want to fly, again.

Forgotten Stars

The fireplace burns with innuendo
Sing Sweet, Seraphim, songs of life's release
Mournings staring out the frosty windows
And Chopin heartstrings from my fingertips
With strains of cinnamon tea and biscuits
Memories offer no consolation
The real world snickers mean encouragement
Let the freak peek from behind open eyes
Retrospection versus reality
Influences dim like afternoon mist
All that remains are lyrical sighs
The perfume of summer in wintertime
Often truth from empathic lips whisper
Enigmatic, words fall apart like dreams
A soul's assentation from darkness to light
As lovely as faded butterfly wings
All I can do is listen and recall
The soundtrack of my forward momentum

UGH

Sky eye blue tee
Because somehow, in it,
I feel less alone
Bury my head in a pillow
And hope to suffocate before I cry
It never works, by the way
Pray for some direction
From whatever Omnipotent Entity
Chooses to answer
*I'm still on cosmic hold
And the choice of music bites*
Seriously, who does that to metal?
Looking for some proof
That not by myself in another fight,
The same battle
I'm tired and lost, I guess
Sigh with an eye roll
I suppose the silver lining is that
If all else fails.
I can threaten people with my head on a stick
That might be fun actually

Uncommon Fire

You called me sister twister
but you turn like a tornado
stirring words and empty emotion
into an inedible buffet that
I can't bear to sit eat from
for fear of poison and hate sauce.
no one counts the cost any more.
it's a lost art to be kind
and not considered a doormat
c'mon kitty kat
you know what I mean
bare your teeth all you wish
but put away your claws.
pause
cause and effect
I got the message long ago but kept trying to
resuscitate a slowly decaying corpse
and hoped it would change back
into the monster I loved
when it awoke
again.

Skin Deep

I starve myself, deprive myself
So you can't see me
Out of sight, out of mind
Peek a boo I'm still here
It's my own failing
And my own damned fault
For letting myself be shoved aside
This time I'm out of care
Humanity is blinded by their own hand
Choosing to look solely at the opaque
Farther down is too far to go
Skin deep is rather shallow and
Eye candy is just empty calories
Certainly not nourishment
Soul food is sustenance for survival
What a sweet treat to find both
Encased in one gilt wrapped gift
Sometimes the true horror lies in the mind refraction
Where no one can escape reality

Naked Bones

Lay like bones
Lying in white wearing my shroud
With my tired eyes closed
Practicing for death
Without the commitment
Crackling bubbles, my watery grave
I still can't breathe,
But stay here anyway
Where I'm finally warm
My solitude is enjoyable but
I wish for company
I could sleep soon
Safe in your arms,
If you were here
I could rest, maybe, unafraid
Happily in Your grasp
I could be infinitely free
If I knew how to be
Who am I, anyway?
I've forgotten or that person has vanished
She's been gone so long but I miss her
She's the key, Emotion's voice
And her Siren songs are raw and real
All because she loves you

Melanie McCurdie

What Made It Real

I miss the soft rain
of your voice
how it would fall like
soothing balm on my
rage, dampening it
to low embers
The laughs over cigarettes
quiet snickers
Belly laughs until our ribs hurt
Silent conversations
Grasping at words to
Say anything,
Struggling and letting it die_
The small, quiet talks
Hearts weeping from our eyes
when it got too big
I wanted to have it all
Not just some, some of the time
Devotion to a dreamh
A lovely dream
I have dreams of my own
and sometimes
Love just isn't enough

Dreaming Minds

the fever pain in my brain will drive me insane
rupture membranes and lacerate my pride
if I bother to try so I hide what's inside
when I should be confiding
but life is confounding and
minds are designed to take pressure
sometimes they crack and the noise of the claque knock
back shatters
fucked up chattering locked up confined
other minds take compression like a fine bowl of smoke
they bottle aggression and spit out diamonds
rare gems that brighten the horizon
I'm no quitter or weak sister mister
badass bitch all day and all night
put your dukes up still willing to fight alright
but bodies are breaking minds quaking
monster is at the door on the floor
and I'm really too tired to right anymore
what's the score?
put me in coach
I'm still ready and steady
goodnight

No Sky

I loved you once
I won't deny it
Damned near idolised you
Certainly, would have bled or died
Stupid youth
It never knows when to sit the fuck down and pay attention.
Blah blah I know everything - you know fuck all
The funny part is that it was true
I did know everything about nothing
And nothing existed except your eyes
The feel of your arms around me
A steady heartbeat still means safety
That's what you taught me
What's the worst part?
It all sucks harder than a ten-dollar whore
But the worst thing is that lessons die hard
I'm less open as I grow colder and
I've become harder as I get older
Time doesn't always heal
Lessons often start to decay before I notice
But even if you knocked on my door
I would still welcome in - welcome you home

Unspoken

All the things I could say:
I am worried
I am trying
I am sad
I am scared
I am hurt
I am pissed off
I feel unloved
I feel unworthy
I feel invisible
I feel lost
I feel abandoned
I love you
I really don't like you
I think I deserve better
I know I deserve better
I gave you everything I had
I gave up dreams for you
I protected you
I trusted you
I TRUSTED YOU
What I will say:
Nothing

Babble

What I really need right now is
someone to sit and hear
listen to me babble.
The herbal life makes things smaller
easier to deal with but
I really need someone
who can love without judgement,
hear my words and help me
try to make some sense of it
of what is stuck in my head
it's stuck in my heart
my throat is mocked, blocked
no sound I'm driven mute
It's fury and passion
wrapped up in a cherry bomb
and stuffed in a pneumatic cannon
that's aimed at my own reflection
I'm helpless to stop it on my own;
What I really need
right now is someone
to just sit and listen

I'm Sorry

I'm human and I don't want to be these days.
I'm real even though you say different
Much as you deny it I have feelings too; I bleed.
Treatments hurt and I hide it
But I'm sorry if it bothers you
that I needed you
.

I'm not ugly and I'm sorry that bothers you too
I've offered to change that.
Regret is the worst thing in the world
We hurt each other so often.
I failed you. But I tried.
It wasn't enough and I'm sorry I'm still here
These days I'm so fucking sorry that
Sometimes it's hard to keep breathing
.

I'm still human and I'm so tired
But I'm still fighting every day
I'm sorry I can't be more of what you expect
I'm in pain and no one who hasn't suffered understands
how you can lay in the dark and think,
I'm just too far gone
I don't think I can anymore.."

Melanie McCurdie

Tears are for Flowers

You see,
There are all of these thoughts
And dandelion fluff mixed up with
Feelings and stupid things like that
So I end up tongue-tied and twisted
Because I can't speak,
Not even a peep
Understand,

It's all about control
Never letting go for one second
Stay diligent! Stay your post, and
I have
But I'm tired of being an empty bottle
That always has to be filled until
There's no room left

And so,
I stuff it down, smile some more
Get bent out of shape inside
Because there's nowhere to run
What else is there to do but hide?
It doesn't matter.
Reconstruction starts over again
More mortar holes to fix
Crumbling passages make one weak
Tears are for flowers
So stop your crying
Rebuilding walls, filling aches
That maybe, one day,
can just crumble away

Sweet Sacrifice

You say, *come, beauty*
Holding your hand out with a smile
A reassuring gesture meant to placate, calm
Yet behind your eyes a gleam
Of misadventure, madness
That glitters like a lecherous jewel
Intent on stealing my heart, that frozen wasteland

Not much grows there
I reply to your quizzical stare
As you pull me closer, and finding no resistance whisper
I will be your undoing
As I slice through the tethers
And emotional duct tape
You use to bind yourself together
I will leave you on the floor
Shaking, bleeding from the shards of shattered dreams

Will I remember?
Those wishfully forgotten dreams, that plague me?
I murmur, feeling your teeth graze my flesh
A silvery shiver that leaves me aquiver, trapped in your eyes
Desires flames roar as the fire animal blazes,
The perfect mixture of pleasure and pain
A Sweet sacrifice paid
To destroy one another
In Love's embrace

Inhuman

Some hate to cry
Not dislike or detest
HATE
I learned that tears are not strength
I learned that
They are a waste of precious fluid, of emotion easy turned
To more creative pursuits
They are a typical stereotype
If you are a woman
You cry at everything
The stereotype proves a truth
A man is viewed as strength
Showing rage, or love, even touched
Rarely seen with a tear
Tears are weakness
They are human
I don't want to be that anymore
Humans hurt and they bleed
They bleed over everything
They're manic depressive madmen
Which is can be good
In more creative pursuits
In life its simpler
You don't feel
You don't care
Tears are a moot point
And you don't have to bleed.

Reactions May Vary

Do you think me pretentious
Or just inane because I refuse to kneel
After a lifetime on my knees
Praying to a nonexistent God
Or bowed to the will of another
I've done my time in Hell

Thank you for not shoving your belief
Down my throat
If I wanted a religious facefuck
I'd google it, so thanks again
If I appear rude, it's because I am being so
Blame it on the snow in California
Or on social media and what have you
But stop asking me to prey to a dead deity
There is no God
.
Maybe once upon a time I could buy it
Now as an adult it could never be
God abandoned me for greener pastures
See ya buhbuye!! He waved hello
To the age'd averages in Florida
Or blew himself up in space
Who the fuck knows
Zealots and factionists come in all shapes and sizes
Even grow in your own backyard,
according to the media mongers,
History speaks volumes if you care to listen
All the religions in the human experience
Started with LOVE
One has to wonder when love became hate

Pills

They make them look so pretty
Brightly coloured like candy
Anyone who has taken antibiotics
Knows this is a baldfaced cheat
They do not taste like jellybeans
They do make a nifty rattle though
Like a lame ass maraca
If you are stuck for accompaniment
They tell lies
Like it'll be quieter
Or you'll be able to think
Or you'll be able to smile
...
...
Quieter would be nice
I think too much so fuck that
Smile ...
Truth is
I don't see much to smile about. I'm trying find that silver lining
And it's an exhausting task
I'm struggling and I've fallen silent because I can't speak
Four words to describe my last effort
Colossal Waste Of Time

Pills.
They lie.
If I listened to them, life would be roses and peaceful
I'd be able to think
I'd have forever to enjoy it too because I'd be in the ground.
They do make a nifty rattle though.

Fantasy

You are watching me
I feel it; I can see it
Your stare sends heat waves
Burning smoldering holes
Our eyes, they meet
Tangle and tussle in the air
Yours blue as the summer sky
A sensory kiss in a glance
A flicker of movement
Invitation
I smile, bite my lip, and nod

Walls the colour of blood feed the desire
Grabbed, - I can't breathe
Locked up tight, unwilling to fight
A hand on my breast
Warm palm over my mouth
As though I'd scream
Back against the wall
Kissing, Tearing, desperately pulling
Heat,
A gasp
There is no preamble
All ahead and deep
Hand holds back the scream
Thrusting desire as though to break bones
Exploding with snarling delight
Warmth inside is molten honey
Panting release and secret sighs
It is all just fantasy

Melanie McCurdie

Seasonal

It's an awkward situation to be in, sitting bareassed
naked on the landing in the middle of the night
with my face in my hands.

I crept downstairs in silence, exhausted to the point of
lunacy now four days into brutal week
of mostly sleepless nights.

And was morose but fine until I saw that fucking lit up
tree covered in decorations and came apart.

The struggle to smile is a battle. My teeth feel stained
and bloodied, my lips bruised from the verbal
skirmishes.

These days. These days. Today, the struggle not to give in
and to stay is a tougher one.

The guilt over even considering death as a viable solution
to insomnia is almost as torturous as the desire.

It's a battle I fight every day, but
I'm still here. I may be weak, in tears, torn as old
butterfly wings, but I am here.

Lyconda Rising

She keeps asking me.
Demanding I tell her the translation
The meaning of the Lycondian Lullaby,
the one that I carved
in the stone wall
below the altar.
As though she's forgotten.
Had she?
I've spoken not a word, and won't
Not since she bound me in this body
In this vessel, trapped,
while the Ancients mutter
The Storms are growing darker
Not the finger of God
But the Fist of Gods
Bent on redemption and destruction
Lyconda Rising
She rises in Corporeal Splendor
And I,
I her willing sacrifice, shiver
Tasting metal and fire in the air
When her lips meet mine
in misguided method
Her trembling smile fades in horror
As Lyconda respires and draws in breath,
But in the carcinogenic burn of her embrace
I gain my freedom, spread my ribs
Lycondian Lullaby, the characters glow
How She Rises, pulling me with Her
With no time to bid goodbye
To the bitch now trapped in the clock

exegesis

You've killed every part
Of my now frigid heart
Once it was full of life
Breathed life into love
It was enough for you to overthrow loyalty for
opportunity
Once upon a time I believed in you
When I was more than simply an automaton
A toy for amusement
A pretty alphabetized garland
of letters on a screen
Just a stupid game

Not real, I can't possibly feel
But I do. And I am.
I'm not just a plaything
My body and mind exist
I may be now nothing more
Than a transparent facsimile
Cellophane. Invisible
A discarded illusion that feeds your fantasy
But each time those emotions flare
Burn. They ache and sting

I want to hate you
The ever pressing desire to cut you out
Be free of the encumbrances
That your existence uses to bind
The ability escapes me.
I cannot do unto you as you have me
And so I suffer heartburn of the soul
And prey each day that fate will quench it
Because I love you still
And would rather die than live knowing
I that I can never be rid of your lies

Maybe

I despise the word desperate
Yet the scrabbly, bitey thoughts
Those that rattle
like rats in a rucksack
Offer no other bon mot in place

Unfortunately, desperation aside,
I'm afraid and dumbstruck,
The daemon stole my tongue -
so easily stolen - but ...

~must you make me twitch ye perpetual devil? ~
I'm trying to be serious so listen
!
ajuster ma couronne

You've been like glue and I love you
What's more, I'm astonished...
Undeserving.

For Sanity's Sake
Would you *please* stop grinning
You mean old thing!
Playing peekaboo on the mirror's edge

I still win.
You're not getting a medal, you know,
For your torturous truth bombs

...
...

Perhaps, on further consideration,
a Purple Heart
For braving teeth and tears,
Unflinchingly. Without judgement.
Maybe

Melanie McCurdie

Flutter

You don't get it
being trapped in your head and trapped in your mind
all corridors and no exits -
nothing but hallways and corners
with no safe place to hide
from the monsters inside me
they induce fear and prison
all my life since then stolen away
like treasure by pirates yo ho Ho but there is no rum
just poison that drips from lips
laced in false truths and honest lies
like it'll never happen again
and I love you and please don't leave
then it's better until it's hell
until the fists
until the wishes for death
you're drowning in brimstone freezing alone
with no fire left in you but by some miracle
an ember survives
or I'm too too stupid to know
that I died long ago
when my expression was taken
I ache to create
put my fingers on cool keys
gentle ivories
let it flow like magic
water into a desiccated soul
it hurts to miss the soundscapes
the release of the notes
a thirst never quenched
it just coughs dust and regret
while I die without an outlet to scream
or a prescience of presence
in a trusted heart that judges not
just listens to the inane
insane babblings of a lost heart
that's tired of wandering

Ripples

                        What a surprise
The harridan cries in my eyes, in my head, no surprise

                      She despises the air that I breathe
                      Suffer her pitiless pithy phrases

        Sardonic bitch, her thoughts leave scars
Open wounds that fill and shimmer but never bleed,
                            every action replay

                      She hands me the knife
                      She holds my hand while I carve
                      Praying for someone to save me
                      No one will come

                      Pray no more, God is dead
                      I still live to suffer the cuts
                      The fractures in my mask widen
                      Wrinkles mark time and I am age'd
                      Too young to be so old and empty

                      I keep saying it can't be but really,
                      Honestly, tonight
                      I would welcome Death
                      As a viable scapegoat
                      A welcome partner
                      I search for relief but I'm looking
                      For someone to just

                      Harridan sighs
                      Spits on the blade
                      She coats it in reasons
                      Same old seasons that drag on
                      She hates me, I know
                      The marks tell the tale
                      Still her bite is more comfortable
                      Than the poison I feed myself.

Melanie McCurdie

<u>Excogitate</u>

I threw away the childish games
The day the first punch was thrown
Admittedly
I haven't seen them coming since
Perpetually punch drunk

And some might think me naïve
Or blind bordering on stupid
But I'm not
I'm just not an open door
If I let you in, you have a home
I don't let many see me
Agoraphobic antisocial
More often than you think
Bet you didn't know

The permanent scars aren't conceivably beautiful
I can barely stand the reflection
I don't fight, I rage inside, where it's quiet
And I can be withdrawn
Where my mask can come off
With no judgement or fear
It's safe there, and I can loathe
Myself. Mores the pity

Don't tell me you love me
Unless you mean it
Those are words I take to heart
I don't speak them unless it's right

I still believe in will-o-wisps and fairy dust, monsters
Magic and Dragons, faefolk and gargoyles
and that squirrels and clowns are evil

I also know this ....
While plausibly these all exist, love does not.
It's a unicorn

The Freebase Song

It happening again
I swear I still feel you
It steals away my air

I swear I still hate you
I want to move forward
Your ghost just won't let me

It laughs at me while I SCREAM

I wish you would fuck off
(Just get away from me)
You smell like death and candy
(The fuck away from me)
You make me want to die
(So get away from me)

Your Theory doesn't fly
Don't kill me with kindness
Then stab me with goodbye

I fucking hate your memory
This can't happen again
I swear I still hate you

Leaving you behind me
I don't feel you anymore
Your ghost just can't stop me
It cries while I SCREAM

Melanie McCurdie

You smell like death and candy
(The fuck away from me)
You make me want to die
(So get away from me)

I fucking hate your memory
Your Theory doesn't fly
Don't kill me kindness
Then stab me with goodbye

Languish

When the thunder rolls
I'm so damned lonely
What I really need
Is someone to hold me
Until I can find
The silver lining
And I can breathe again
.

The rain is falling again
(Just keeps fallin)
Reminding me again
(The past keeps calling)
Reminds me of you
(I just can't change)
Reminds me of Sin
(Let's sin again)
.

I lie here empty
Not for survival
Feeling so helpless
My heart like a stone
When I was breathing
You were beneath me
There's no air here alone
....
....
The Lightning crashes
I'm so damned tired
The idea fashes
Your memory haunts me
I can't find that door
That door to forever
When can I feel you again
.

The rain is falling again
(Just keeps fallin)
Reminding me again

Melanie McCurdie

(Past keeps calling)
Reminds me I'm wrong
(I can't fucking change)
I want your Sin
(Let's sin again)
.

I lie here naked
Just for survival
Feeling so desperate
My heart like a flame
I might be alive
No way to know now
There's no air here alone
.

(It's raining again)
There is no air
Want you to scream
(Scream my name)
Let's sin again

*_Happy Place_*

Lights, bright shining in my eyes
I want to murder everyone in the room
The incessant chatter grading on my nerves
Lost in thought, I drift away
To a quieter darker place

I sit alone at the bar
Legs crossed
In silhouette, in the shadows
Sipping my wine and watching the people
Biding my time

How mindless they seem
The wine clings thickly to the inside of the glass
Catching the light, it's sparkles
Darkest red, clings like blood

I'm not alone
The heavyweight of a stare interrupts my observations
A glance to my right tells me much
As though my gaze is enough to provoke movement
And does

I lick the oaken blackberry taste
From my lips, smiling slightly at the widening if your eyes
As I sweep my tongue across my finger

The last remnants sweet, alive
Alive as you are,
The sharp edge taste of your lips achingly soft
My teeth slide through like a hot knife through butter
Your soul through my lips tastes like chocolate
Your pain is my pleasure;
You stab me with your engorged weapon
With your hand up my throat

Melanie McCurdie

My smiling gasp releasing you
And I watched the blood drip down your chin
Teeth coloured The colour of agony

Glittering in the dim light, in the shadows
The forbidden union of creatures
Forgotten in the darkness of passion
The purest desire, I Die, once again
Burned as the Phoenix, ablaze to ashes once again
And feel your molten fire burn within me, I rise
Awaken

Lights bright in my eyes
Voices, incessant chattering alerting me
I am not Alone.

A Grim Affair

The bubbles crackle like the fresh falling snow
on the fire burning out of control just across the road
and this is what she
she replayed in her mind as she watched the fire dance
sparkle with the shadows on the ceiling of the bathroom
oh the sensation of flying, so sure she is flying
the sensation of pleasure so intense
that she bites her hand
he's gone but his hand is her own as he fucks herself
she writhes against it in abandon shouting his name

with no shame

– no nothing but the need fulfilled
she cries in silence
at the storm inside because she knows it's only her mind
and not his hand not him,
it can't be ever again. he's gone
he'd left her
abandoned in a new definition
she is alone and for always
but she swears she can smell his cologne on her pillow
feel his hands on her hips
lips on her lips
hips
tongue
it feels like him and she can't help but moan in protest

he's dead

she still wears his blood on her hands and her face
he promised she grinds alone in her mind she stutters
paces in places well-worn in her padded visceral cell
but his tongue in her, cobwebs and cunnydust
and his fingers scrabbling like creatures
full and gushing eyes shut tight riding the waves

Melanie McCurdie

denial
desire
vernal
carnal
then a new a fullness, a new warmth, a tsunami

but he's gone and sunk deep in pieces where I left him

while her body dies over and over
she sighs over and over

axe then chainsaw
I cut him
it's he
him
She smells his blood
sex, earth and hell
oh my god
what the
no
*get **off***
*get **out***
*it **hurts***

*it **hurts*** but delicious
his movements are vicious and he's dead but inside of
her
the swell and the ocean
his groans
animals feasting
she remembers the reason she feels him so close
then she laughs out loud with release

I ate him

Poison

It drips like clear sugar
Sliding
Drooling
like pearls, desire
Slowly down to hang
Off the edge
Growing pregnant
Dripping. falling
Pooling on the ground
At my feet
From my pen

Poison
Sweetest delight
Lethal, it kills
Slow and with purpose
Like oil in water
It swirls and coats
Seeping into each
Crevice, slowly
Devouring, licking
Along the edges
Searching for an opening
An entry

Delights, shivers
Licks and bites
Screaming desire
It eats, devours
Starts fires, burning
Holes, fraying the edges
Whispering half-truths
No truths
Fangs poke ravaged holes
In my heart,
Cutting the strings
Used to sew it back together

Melanie McCurdie

Edges still swollen
From the rusted needle
Catch it in a jar
Watch it darkle
Sparkle
Delight

A genie in a bottle
Should I rub it
Stroke the glass
Of its prison
Would it appear
Grab me about the throat?
Pin me to the wall
Have its way with me?
Or bow to my will
Ready to please me

Vacant Rose

It's easier in the dark.
Alone doesn't feel quite so isolating
Wet cheeks go unnoticed
Somehow, the bleakness seems a comfort
Not unlike a pair of warm arms.

She doesn't know I'm watching, lost in her rain cloud
I'm positive that she'd prefer an embrace
To the cold silence

There she sits, cross-legged, nude,
Tragic beauty she cries, face in a pillow
The mirror covered in linen
I know she is wishing for the strength
For the courage set right the horror show
That she sees in the mirror reflection

But, much like me, she's a coward
A loser done up on codeine and weed
Practically paralysed, poor thing
And all in an effort to achieve peace
Much like me, she's achieving nothing close to it.

These are the nights I can't help but hate
Because what other choice is there
I can hardly barge in, now can I?
Invading her misery by pulling her close
I want to take it away, if she'd let me, if I could,
Instead I watch her turn it inward
It's a simpler method to live with
Mechanisms to emancipation
I write the steps to her freedom

It's all about weights and measures
The balance is off; the telemetry is fucked
Knowing so doesn't calm a racing heart
Or stop the tearing desire to howl

Melanie McCurdie

Soon, so soon, Impatience cries

I'm sick of waking each day
Gasping because I'm dying of suffocation
It all comes from bottling
The anticipation is agony

She rises, long and lean
Her lips rippling as she chants the same ugly litany
Telling herself that it's stupid to be in fear of nothing
idiotic to be afraid of long dead monsters
What are you, 12?
Trembling with fear like a child, no desire in the dark
Are you so desperate to be swept away?
Just take the pills and shut up

Pacing, bare flesh flashing, her hair flies static
Staring out at the street below
Tonight its defenestration she battles

I know how she thinks
I know all this as well as I know my own heart
The idea of that beautiful body
Splattered like red velvet vomit

Horrified and aroused
Blood spilled spells oxygen.
The weight of biology is lifted
Swiftly slipping to press against the glass
She stares, pondering and
My temperature burns hotter, the daemon salivates,
Its venom fills my mouth
Such a glorious gluteus maximus
It calls my palms with a sirens wail
So long she's teased me
Pleading for release from her glass tower
Tonight her prayers are answered
Blood is life.

I'm so tired of bleeding.
Now it's her turn

ABOUT THE AUTHOR

I am a Canadian based writer who resides in Calgary, Alberta and am blessed with two challenging boys. A Warrior Mom to Sam, aged 14 and DaveyB, aged 10, administrator with The Twisted Path Group, rabid supporter of Independent Film and Publications, and a horror junkie with a taste for words, and bloodsauce.

Made in the USA
Middletown, DE
02 June 2018